Fight or Fright?

A Reactive Dog Guardian's Handbook

JAY GURDEN

Copyright © 2019 Jay Gurden

All rights reserved. No part of this book may be reproduced or used in any manner without the written permission of the copyright owner except for the use of quotations in a book review

ISBN: 1795059478
ISBN-13: 9781795059473

CONTENTS

	Special Thanks	i
	Foreword	ii
1	Introduction	1
2	What is reactivity?	9
3	How do I know if my dog is reactive?	18
4	What does reactivity do to the dog?	25
5	What does reactivity do to the owner?	33
6	The importance of support	42
7	Right type of trainer	50
8	Practical steps to emotional peace	58
9	Prevention over cure	67
	About the author	75

SPECIAL THANKS

There are a number of people without whom this book could not have happened. My family, in particular my long suffering husband, have tolerated many hours of me sitting in corners muttering to myself. None of this would have happened if I had not come across a Facebook post about a course in reactive dog behaviour. That link led me to Canine Principles. I am incredibly grateful to the entire team there for providing such great courses and student support that I became inspired to learn as much as I could. I have also been very fortunate to benefit from the inspiration and support of the wonderful Sally Gutteridge who, I am thrilled to say, has written a foreword for this book. Huge thanks also go to Fiona Gemmell for her editing skills, smoothing out the clunky edges of some of the prose, and dealing with my sometimes cavalier preposition positioning!

The final thanks go to the one that truly inspired this book, and he can't even read! Finn has been the most complicated dog that I have ever known. Ultimately that has made him the most rewarding when we have made even the smallest step forward. Because of him, I know more now than I ever would have imagined.

FOREWORD

What a wonderful insight into life with a dog who needs extra support. Jay not only covers how the dog feels but provides a candid and honest account of how it affects us to share our lives with a dog who finds the world intimidating. Packed with empathy and understanding, this book is like a discussion with a friend who knows exactly what you experience when caring for a dog who needs special help.

Based in facts and delivered with compassion throughout; this book will leave you feeling less alone with your dog and more part of a bigger group. Welcome to a tribe of dog guardians where we all have the wellbeing of our dogs at heart, which is sometimes overwhelming but always rewarding.

Keep going with your dog, they are resoundingly worth it; and Jay's words will help you along the way.

Sally Gutteridge..

1 INTRODUCTION

Most people, when they envisage having a dog in the family, have an idea of what life will be like once the new family member has arrived. A playful, friendly ball of fur who enjoys romps around the countryside with human and canine friends. Every person and dog welcomed with a wag of the tail and maybe a soft doggy kiss. It makes for a very appealing image.

What happens can be very different.

Very few people knowingly picture adding a dog to their family unit that finds the world a difficult place. None of us sets out to be the one holding a lead, the other end of which is barely hanging on to a furiously snarling, foaming and barking bundle of hackles and teeth.

Sadly, for some people and their dogs this is the reality. For many in this position, that initial moment can be shocking, even frightening. With the response that such behaviours often get from other, uninitiated people in the vicinity, it can be humiliating as well.

Welcome to the emotional rollercoaster that is life as the guardian of a reactive dog.

Inspiration for this book came from the unexpected, huge reaction to a post that I wrote on my blog Blue Merle

Minion. My inbox filled with comments and messages from people that completely understood what I had written, full of relief that they could see other people exist that understand what it is like to be the person on the other end of that lead. That article is in part the very basics of sections of this book, in an effort to show more people that they are definitely not alone, to help them understand what both sides of the partnership between human and dog are going through, but also to provide some details on how to go about improving the situation.

If you are reading this because you are at this point, with a dog that on occasions turns into a whirling, snarling dervish, then I hope to help point you in the direction of help, support and ways to improve the situation so that you and your dogs can have the best life possible together. By sharing my experiences, and the sources of help and advice that I managed to locate, my aim is to aid guardians and handlers of reactive dogs to reduce stress in both their dogs and themselves as rapidly as possible.

How it all began – emotional toll of reactivity

By way of further introduction, this first chapter includes the text of the blog post that started off this project. The subject had been on my mind for a while before writing this article, largely because I have been so fortunate in the people and places that I made my way to at the beginning of my journey with a reactive dog more by luck than judgement. I have seen so many people in these places (mostly Facebook related, as so many things seem to be these days) posting for the first time about the relief they feel at having found people that understand, that can sympathise and – in my mind more importantly – empathise with that horribly lost, confused feeling.

When you first realise that your dog is reactive, you can feel utterly despondent, isolated, desperate and helpless. This book is designed to show you that none of these feelings have to be permanent. Very few books or articles that I discovered while first looking into the subject of reactive dogs when the issue came up for me even really mentioned the effects it was having on me. The technical literature is largely aimed at helping the dog. This is, of course, a hugely important part of improving things. However, having been there myself, I now fully believe that the owners and handlers need help as well. After all, how can we help our dogs if we are not in a good emotional state and able to remain calm in potentially tricky situations? How can we expect our fearful dogs to trust us to keep them safe in scary situations if they can sense that we are scared or annoyed? The human on the other end of the lead needs to be able to understand how they are physically and emotionally affected by reactivity just as much as their dog is.

This post contains my story. How I discovered that reactive dogs existed, and what brought me to this point of now studying canine coaching and behaviour and writing a book on the subject of reactive dogs and their guardians. It is written with total honesty, including the things that went wrong during his young puppy days, both the things that were out of my control and the things that I got wrong through not knowing better. Our story began when my dog was eight weeks old, but the difficulties of reactivity can crop up in dogs of any age, dependent on a number of factors which will come up later.

The Emotional Toll of Reactivity.

Get a dog, they said. It'll be fun, they said. Think of all those great, social dog walks, they said.

So why am I stumbling around a field at 4.30 in the morning?

I've had a number of dogs over the years. All have had their distinct personalities, but all were fairly easy going, and liked meeting people and going to places. Owning a dog meant that people would sometimes smile as we walked past them in the street, children would come up and ask if they could fuss them, and our dogs loved all of the attention.

And then along came Finn.

Finn is the most adorable goofball of a dog at home with the people he knows and trusts. That extends to a grand total of 5 people. I had never heard the term 'reactive dog' when we picked up the little ball of fluff at 8 weeks old and brought him home. I knew that some people had 'aggressive' dogs but I would never have one of those. Surely aggressive dogs must have been abused, or poorly raised, right?

Finn is something of a perfect storm of what can cause reactivity. His mother is a very nervous dog, and he has definitely inherited that. He's very jumpy around strange noises and the unfamiliar. Through illness, he missed out on socialisation during the critical learning period. When we were then later playing catch up, I will admit I pushed him a bit hard to meet new things, having never had a dog quite as nervous in nature as him and not knowing what I was risking. And lastly, just to really put the nail in things, he was bitten by another dog out on a walk.

I had no idea what I was looking at as he started to shy away from things. I tried my best to reassure and encourage him to check out the new things but nothing seemed to work. And then, finally, it happened. He full on reacted, lunging and barking at some other people walking their dogs. I will never, ever forget the look they gave me.

There are any number of articles that you can find about how to reassure and help your reactive dog. There are far, far fewer that in any way prepare you for the emotional rollercoaster that is being the owner or handler of a reactive dog.

I'm going to be brutally honest here. I love the very bones of Finn, he is the most beautiful dog to look at. He sleeps on my bed, keeps me company wherever I go in the house and is always up for a game in the garden or an ear rub. As I'm typing this, he's using my foot as a pillow while he snoozes. I will never pass this dog on to someone else because of his issues. He is reactive to all dogs, and all people with the exception of a very small circle which consists of me, my husband, my mum, my sister and one of my brothers. Everyone else is loudly told to go away. He's utterly terrified of children. So no, I would never pass him on. There have been times, however, when I will admit that I wished I'd never set eyes on him. I have cried more tears over this one dog than over any other animal I've ever had, even the ones that I've had to say that permanent goodbye to. Because of Finn, I have been patronised, pitied, sworn at and despised.

So we walk at 4.30 in the morning. It's a lovely time of day in summer, light and cool but with no one else around to worry about as we ramble over the field. Less so now as we leave and get home in the dark. It does mean though that we only have to dodge a couple of people out on their way to work early or for an early morning jog. We're all largely used to each other, so I just move out of their way and use the encounter as a little training session and we've gone from massive handfuls of food being sprinkled on the ground to one treat at a time, looking calmly at the moving torch of the other person between each treat. When the weather gets worse, we will start going out mid-morning, once the school run is finished, and start letting him see a few more people. Will he react? There's a chance it will happen at some point, but there are some things I have learned to help me cope since first discovering that I have a reactive dog.

There is a good chance you will cry at some point. It happens. Nobody sets out to have a dog and not be able to have those lovely sociable walks with that dog playing happily with friends. I've been dealing with this for over a year now, and still have days where it all weighs me down and I crack. Don't try and hold it in. Concentrate on the fact that you know what the issue is and can work on it.

Let the emotions out so that the next time you take your reactive dog out, you can leave the negative emotions behind and focus on your dog and what you need to do to help them learn to cope.

Get help. Whether it is a good trainer/behaviourist (and it DOES need to be a good, positive one for this issue), books written by said good trainers or behaviourists or the help of a community of people that understand what you and your dog are going through (Reactive Dogs UK were an absolute lifeline for me) it is vital to find yourself advice and a support network. Living with a reactive dog is an emotional situation, and one that you cannot get through on your own and remain sane.

Educate yourself on reactivity, the causes and the things that you can do to help. There are courses that help you understand what is going on in your reactive dog's brain and why they do the things that they do. Canine Principles have an amazingly detailed and informative course in Canine Reactive Behaviour that I would thoroughly recommend if you want to understand the science behind reactivity and fear aggression. A couple of UK based dog trainers that write knowledgeably and accessibly about reactivity are Janet Finlay who runs the Canine Confidence Academy and Beverley Courtney of Brilliant Family Dog. Another excellent read (and overnight bestseller when released on Amazon!) is written by Canine Principles founder and mentor to many (including me) Sally Gutteridge, titled 'Inspiring Resilience in Fearful and Reactive Dogs' and can be found on Amazon.

Don't let the attitudes of others get you down. Concentrate on you and your dog. Remember that everything you are doing is for the good of your dog, and what others think if you suddenly veer off and 'ninja' behind some bushes on seeing another dog approaching, cross the road or about turn and head home on seeing something that you know your dog is scared of really does not matter. The most important thing is that you know your dog can trust you to keep them safe and keep them away from the things that scare them. The more you do that, the more your dog will come to know it and trust you to do so.

Finally, what I think is the most important thing to remember: your dog behaves the way he does because he's scared. Reactivity stems from fear. It's not being aggressive for the sake of it, it's your dog trying to frighten off the scary thing before it can get close enough to hurt him. It doesn't matter if it seems like a ridiculous thing to be scared of. We once had a situation where Finn reacted to something and I couldn't for the life of me see what it was, as there were no dogs and no people in sight. I watched and watched him as I tried to work out what he was scared of so that we could find a way past it. What was it? A bin on someone's driveway that was 6 feet away from where it normally was. It was different, so it was wrong and going to get him. I admit, I laughed for a second as it seemed so ridiculous to me. But then I realised it didn't matter what I thought, to Finn it was a monster because it had moved. The fear was very real to him.

Living with a reactive dog is never going to be easy. It can be rewarding as they come to trust you more, but it can be completely draining as well. There are times when it feels like one step forward then two steps back. Stick with it, accept the fact that it's going to be tough but remember that when you do make progress, the feeling will be amazing and it will have happened because of the work that you have put in.

As a friend reminds me on the days I'm feeling down, it's not the easy dogs that make us good handlers and trainers, but the difficult ones. The complicated ones. Finn has been the reason for many, many tears but he has also been the reason for some incredible highs. Because of Finn, I found some amazing groups of people that have supported me in my journey with him and with dogs in general. In my case, my reactive dog is the reason for a complete life change, for putting me on this new route in my life. I will always be grateful to him for that.

2 WHAT IS REACTIVITY?

Reactivity may be a new word for some. It certainly was a new word for me when I was first confronted with the fact that I owned what at the time I called at the time a 'difficult' dog.

The Oxford English Dictionary defines reactive as 'showing a reaction', and reaction as 'something done or experienced as a result of an event or situation'. The concept of reactivity in dogs takes the idea of showing a reaction a little further. A reactive dog is showing a reaction above and beyond the norm, exaggerated compared to how the average dog would react in the same situation.

To get the subject out of the way at the very beginning, let's look at what reactivity is not. Reactivity has absolutely nothing to do with dominance. A dog that lunges and barks at something is not trying to show dominance or mark his place over it. Simply put, that is not the way that dogs work. The dominance myth is a pervasive one that simply will not die, aided as it is by some people that call themselves trainers, but are stuck blindly following false information based on outdated, flawed studies on wolves.

A brief history of the dominance theory.

In 1947 a scientist named Rudolf Schenkel published a scientific paper entitled 'Expression Studies on Wolves'. This paper detailed the study of a group of wolves that lived in a zoo in Switzerland, and concluded from observing their behaviour that members of the group fought to be the leader, the 'alpha' wolf. Schenkel's study represented the first time behavioural studies had been undertaken on wolves, and Schenkel drew comparisons between wolves and domestic dogs a number of times throughout the publication. There are major flaws in Schenkel's conclusions from observing these wolves but unfortunately, although science has moved on, the concept of the alpha wolf striving for dominance and that behaviour being replicated in the dog, the supposed little wolf living in our homes, just will not die.

How was Schenkel wrong? He was observing a group of wolves, after all. How could what he saw in them not be valid? It is very simple. The group he observed in the zoo bore very little resemblance to how wolves live in the wild. In their natural environment, wolves live in family groups. The breeding pair are the parents or close relatives of the rest of the pack, and keep control of the pack in the same way any parent would. The wolves in the zoo group were unrelated, and lived in a fenced compound much smaller than the territory that would be covered to encounter unfamiliar wolves in the wild. In that situation, the wolves were bound to fight, and were never going to behave in the same way as wolves in their natural wild environment and family groups would.

It is true that the domestic dog is closely related to the modern Grey Wolf, sharing all but a fraction of their DNA according to genetic research. There is ongoing debate whether they are part the same species (Canis lupus familiaris) or a species in their own right (Canis familiaris). Grouping animals into species is often based in part on whether the different varieties can successfully breed together. The existence of wolfdog hybrids show that this is the case, but the paths each animal has taken in the last few thousand years have been markedly different. While the exact way in which the dog became domesticated is not known for sure, what we do know is that they come from a common ancestor with the Grey Wolf diverging at some time between 16,000 and 35,000 years ago, and started being domesticated somewhere around 15,000 years ago as far as can be calculated from archaeological evidence. During the time that has passed since then, generation after generation of selective breeding by humans has resulted in a huge variety of types of dog, particularly since the breeding boom that took place in the Victorian era, and the interest since then in certain breeds. The dog is the mammal most varied in form on the face of the planet. Compare the Chihuahua to the Great Dane – both are the same species but are very different in appearance. There are a huge number of dog breeds in the world, more than 350, of all shapes and sizes. One thing that all these breeds of domestic dog have in common and the modern wolf does not is the fact they have been selectively bred for human purposes for thousands of years, and bred to live alongside us. That alone gives more than enough reason to treat the two as very different animals.

To see further see why using dominance theory as a basis for training dogs, in particular for reactive dogs, is a bad idea, we must now look at the basis of what reactivity actually is: fear.

I know that might sound strange to the person that started reading because their dog has been growling, snarling and lunging, looking for all the world as if they want to rip apart whatever is in front of them. Nevertheless, the root cause is still fear. The dog showing overt fearful body language is much easier to recognise as being scared, as they try to hide behind their owner from the scary thing, or even try to bolt away home. The dogs that may suddenly slam on the brakes just a few paces outside their own front door and refuse to go any further on their walk ensuring they will not encounter something they are frightened of. In both cases, the essential cause is the same. Both these dogs are scared and trying to deal with their fear, keeping themselves safe, in the most efficient, safest way possible for themselves.

There is a similarity between these two seemingly different behaviours that might not be readily apparent. In both cases, the dog is trying to create distance from the scary object or person. Hiding behind someone or something or running away are both obvious methods to increase distance. The dog showing aggressive behaviours is also trying to create distance not, as some people may think, actually trying to attack unless all other choice has been taken away from them. The idea of these behaviours is to make themselves look scary, dangerous and terrifying and make the scary thing go away before it can get close enough to hurt the dog. It becomes a little clearer if we give this aggression its full title of fear aggression. This also helps to explain why some dogs can be fine off lead but react when on their lead, or maybe seem a bit less reactive off lead but react often when on lead. The option to run away and create distance has been removed and so they feel forced to use defensive displays towards triggers.

But sometimes he's fine and others he's crazy!

One of the most confusing things about living with a reactive dog – particularly when the canine stress signals are still a foreign language to us - is that they can seem so unpredictable in how they react to triggers. Some days your dog will walk past the yapping dog hurling itself at the fence of the garden at the end of the road as if he doesn't have a care in the world. The next day he has grown two feet taller and is dragging you along the street, hackles waving high in the air, and growling constantly. Both days have involved the same walk, on the same route. How can two days show such varied behaviour in a dog?

In training and behaviour language, any stimulus that causes a dog to become stressed and display stress signals is called a trigger – they trigger behaviours, such as avoidance, displacement or creating distance between the dog and the threat in the case of fear driven triggers. Different dogs will have different triggers. The same dog may have a number of different triggers. My reactive dog for instance is triggered by all dogs, although large fluffy white ones or small terriers are particularly disliked. He is also triggered by strangers and the sound that extending ladders make when they rattle up and down or are carried. His final (and most major trigger) is children. He also has quite a high chase drive, wanting to chase small furry animals like squirrels and rabbits. He is a Border Collie, so chasing and herding is a normal drive for him, something that he finds rewarding and exciting. Some days he can be calm enough that he can see a child in the distance with nothing more than interest. Another day, just hearing them somewhere nearby can have him in meltdown. Why the difference?

Imagine a scenario for me. You are in the supermarket and get into a queue to pay for your shopping. You may not have much, and anticipate getting out of there smoothly, without hassle. Someone cuts in line in front of you. It is annoying, but they only have a couple of items and give you a big friendly smile. It really is not that big a deal, so although it could be considered annoying, you leave it and avoid the aggravation.

Let us rewind now to earlier in the day...

You walk out of the house to see that you have a flat tyre. How annoying!

Someone cuts you up at the roundabout. Clearly they are an idiot but no damage done.

Every traffic light seems to go red as you are on your way. This 'quick trip' to the shop is taking forever.

In the car park, the only space left is on the far side of the car park, next to someone that cannot park their car properly within the lines so it is hanging over into your space. This means that you have to squeeze in very carefully and just hope you will be able to get back in your car when you come to leave.

You start making your way around the shop and it becomes clear that you have 'that' trolley – the one with a mind of its own and absolutely no intention of being steered anywhere meaning your back and shoulders are getting really sore.

Then, to cap it all off, someone cuts you up in line and gives you this big over cheerful smug grin as they do so. That is just the last straw and you explode at them.

Anyone looking on would likely say 'They just went off on one out of nowhere!'

Welcome to the concept of trigger stacking. Any one of the things that happened on the way to the store or during your shopping trip is annoying to have happen, but add them all together and it is just too much. Every one of those things that has caused you some annoyance lingers in the system for a little while, and that means that the effect is building up. One or two of those occurrences before the queue jumper at the store might have meant that you were left irritated but did not fly off the handle at the person barging in, but the added effect of all of them took you beyond what you could stand without losing it – it took you beyond your reaction threshold.

Dogs are no different.

Each trigger that the dog has will have a certain value. Some things he will find scarier than he will others. As mentioned above, triggers also have a cumulative effect, because of the way that mammals' bodies deal with stress.

This means that if your dog has encountered a few triggers on his walk before getting to the home of the yapping, fence-charging dog, he just does not have the capacity to deal with another trigger. He has reached the threshold of things that he can cope with on any given day and so he reacts, lunging and barking at the fence. The dog is trigger stacked on this particular day, and trigger stacking is what causes that apparent unpredictability in a dog's reactivity.

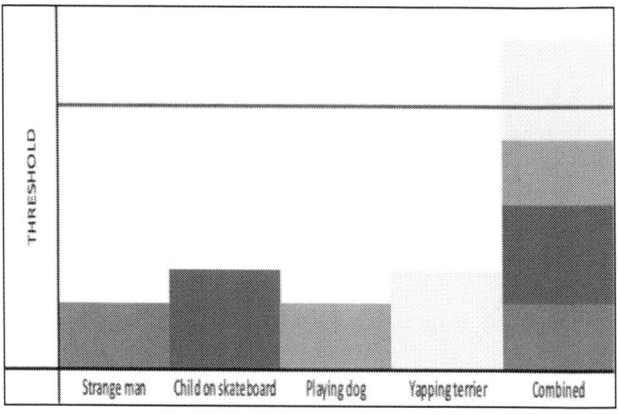

Each of the first four columns on the diagram above represent an individual trigger, each of which the dog can cope with in isolation, or even two or three in combination. Stress is cumulative. Your dog might cope well with the strange man that walks past as you leave the house. He might have a bit of a look at the laughing child on the skateboard coming out of the local play area right on front of you. He stops for a moment and stares at the dog playing with a ball on the other side of the fence, but when you speak to him he breaks his attention and comes with you. Then the terrier starts jumping up and down on the other side of the garden fence and yapping and your dog just explodes. Out of nowhere, he is barking and lunging at the fence. Except if you go back through the previous steps it is not out of nowhere. Each thing your dog could cope with in isolation, even two in a row without being too stressed. The third encounter took him to the limits of what he could tolerate, and the fourth pushed him way over threshold.

Another way to explain this concept is the 'spoon theory', often used to describe how people deal with chronic pain and illness. The theory also works well to explain how dogs can become overloaded with triggers. On any given day, your dog has a certain number of spoons in his mental repository that correspond with the resilience he has to deal with triggers that he might encounter, and those spoons are all he gets to cope with his day. Every trigger takes a certain number of spoons away from the dog, depending on how much fear it provokes in the dog. At some point, if he encounters more triggers, your dog will run out of spoons so has no capacity to deal with any more triggers, and will go over threshold and react.

A phrase that I encountered a few times early in my reactivity journey sums up the important thing to remember when it comes to looking at your life with a reactive dog: *remember that your dog is not giving you a hard time. He is having a hard time.* That one phrase perfectly sums up life for a fearful dog. There is no spite or anything negative directed towards the guardian in reactivity, he is not being awkward or trying to show you up. Something in his world right at that second in time is something that he finds it almost impossible to cope with, and he just wants that thing to go away.

There can be some confusion with dogs that go crazy on lead, barking, growling and standing up on their back legs against the lead when they see another dog, but are then possibly able to greet and play with the other dog if it is not upset by their display and they are able to get close. These dogs are more likely to be what are known as 'frustrated greeters' who want to go and say hello to all of the other dogs, but are not necessarily very good at the social cues and etiquette required to socialise with other dogs. While not technically reactivity, some of the same techniques can help frustrated greeters learn to be calmer around other dogs.

3 HOW DO I KNOW IF MY DOG IS REACTIVE?

What is my dog scared of?

The list of things that might scare a dog is immense. All dogs are, after all, individuals. The things that dogs can be frightened of is almost as varied as the dogs themselves. Common fears include other dogs, unknown people, and strange or loud noises. The only way to be sure what the problems might be for any individual dog is to watch them, learn what their body language means so that you can tell when they first become uncomfortable.

Canine Communication

As much as we might wish, our dogs cannot speak to tell us what is wrong. They have to tell us, to communicate their feelings and needs through body language and a limited range of vocalisations. Canine body language is a huge subject, and can be very intimidating to contemplate in the beginning. The benefit of taking the time to get a good grounding in it cannot be emphasised enough. There is an app available called Dog Decoder available for smartphones, both for Android and iPhone, which can give an easy to reference on the spot guide on how to interpret the signals the dogs around you may be giving off. There are also a number of photographic guides available, which are well worth the purchase price and some time spent studying for a more in-depth level of knowledge. Very small, subtle differences can mean that the dog is communicating very different things. Taking a while to observe and learn what is normal body language for your dog so any changes can be quickly spotted is highly recommended. As always, remember that all dogs are individual, and so there may be slight variations in what constitutes their normal, relaxed body language and, indeed, any body language being displayed to indicate how the dog is feeling at that moment in time.

Breed and any alterations in appearance will have an enormous effect on body language and communication. Ear and tail position will obviously be affected if they have been altered. Tail docking has largely fallen out of favour, and theoretically should not happen in the UK outside of certain circumstances involving the breeding of working dogs that may be considered likely to injure their tails. Sadly, there are always unscrupulous people who will dock certain breeds regardless, as some people still do not want to contemplate having a dog of these breeds with a full tail. Ear cropping is definitely banned in the UK. It is of no health benefit at all, so does not even have the claim to being necessary that tail docking tenuously has, but is purely for aesthetic purposes. This practice of chopping off as much as a third of the ear and then binding it up for several weeks after this removal is designed to make the relevant breed of dogs look a certain way, particularly more aggressive. It is not difficult to imagine that dogs that are either bred to or altered to look more aggressive may well have more difficulties with their interactions with other dogs for example. Any dog that is made to look aggressive may well prompt defensive responses from other dogs, and this may then go on to make the poor cosmetically altered dog suspicious of and defensive towards other dogs in a pre-emptive move. These alterations can also make it difficult for human observers to read the dog's signals if they are not used to seeing dogs that are altered in these ways.

The other factors involved in how appearance alters the dog's signals include colour, skin appearance and hair. Colour is more of an issue in dog to dog communication – many dogs find black dogs difficult in terms of reading facial expressions, so for dogs that are reactive to other dogs, it is quite common to find that black dogs are a particular issue. Lots of loose skin as in dogs such as the Shar Pei, particularly around the mouth like in some jowly breeds, may make important mouth movements such as tight lips or lip wrinkles difficult to observe. Lots of hair may obscure ear or facial movements, or make it very difficult to see if the dog is attempting to raise his hackles.

Devote some time to watching your dog in all kinds of situations and learn how he tells the world that he is happy and relaxed, and spotting the signs that he is starting to be uncomfortable in a situation will become much easier.

How to tell your dog is fearful

The picture that comes to mind when discussing reactive dogs, and also the startling one that is often the first obvious sign to someone that their dog is having difficulties, is the most extreme and impossible to miss. Once you have witnessed a dog pulling at the end of a lead, often so hard that they are standing on their back legs choking themselves on their collar, teeth flashing and foaming at the mouth as they snarl, growl and bark, you have no doubt that there is a problem. This is the point at which many people will seek help, often worried by the fact their dog has behaved in this manner seemingly out of nowhere. The truth is that their dog will have been communicating their discomfort for a while by the time such an extreme reaction happens. There is a saying that dogs can talk, but only to those that can listen. This is very true, as only those that have learned to read canine body language will be able to understand. Fortunately, there are an ever-growing number of sources through which we can educate ourselves on what our canine companions are telling us.

When we can see the first signs of our dogs becoming uncomfortable with situations, we can learn when to intervene, change direction, head for home or whatever else is needed at that time for the mental and emotional wellbeing of both dog and handler. The initial stress signals dogs display are very subtle, but once you have learned to recognise them, it becomes easy to see when your dog is starting to become worried, and the more overt reactions that cause consternation and upset to dog, handler and others around can be avoided.

Things that the handler needs to look out for to tell if a dog in their care could be unhappy includes signals such as avoidance behaviours, turning their head and looking away or trying to hide. A dog lagging behind and walking slowly, or reluctant to walk at all may well be avoiding potential trouble.

One often missed by humans is the quick flick of the nose with the tongue tip or lick of the lips. Yawning is a method of stress release that is not immediately recognisable to people.

Look at your dog's eyes (although never stare into them, as this is extremely confrontational to a dog, and will make matters worse) – if there is a lot of white showing, known as whale eye, the dog may well be stressed.

Ears that are positioned back are a good way to tell, and if flattened right back the dog is probably under a lot of stress. This is less obvious in dogs with long ears, but they will instead clamp their ears tight against the side of the head, as flattening them backwards is not possible.

A crouched body position with the head held low is one of the easiest signals to read as the dog is clearly making themselves smaller to decrease any appearance they may have of being a threat to anyone or anything.

Following a stressful situation, the dog may shake his entire body from nose to tail, literally shaking off the stress.

A tail that is positioned lower than normal, coupled with an arched back denotes stress in the animal, and the tail tucked right under the body between the hind legs is a very clear sign in many dogs. The dog getting close to a fear aggression display may give off a warning signal by holding his tail slightly raised and straight with the body leaning forward in an attempt to push the threat backwards.

Sometimes it may seem as if your dog has strange timing in what he chooses to do. A thing that you know he is unsure of may be approaching and suddenly he sits down and has a scratch, or starts furiously sniffing at a patch of grass for example. These are known as displacement behaviours and are the dog trying to communicate to whatever is coming that they are not a threat, and please just pass on by and leave them alone.

As the stress levels rise, we may start to see the dog panting, tongue lolling. This 'spatulate' tongue, where it hangs long out of the mouth, much wider at the tip and possibly curling up is known by some, in conjunction with a wide, exaggerated facial expression, as a 'clown face' although some breeds can look remarkably similar when not under stress (particularly seen in the Staffordshire Bull Terrier), or after intense exercise. Heavy panting unless you know the dog has just been exercising hard should be viewed with suspicion of stress. The lips are long and tense, and as the dog feels more under threat may be drawn back to show the teeth as a warning. The dog's eyes will show small, contracted pupils and a hard stare, accompanied with furrowed brows. The piloerection response will be seen, more commonly known as the hackles being raised. Hair is held erect in a line following the midline of the dog's back, often seen more clearly over the shoulders and rump of the dog. Strictly speaking, this is not always a sign that an aggressive display will follow as it can mark a range of things in dogs: stimulation, interest, being startled and arousal as well as fear. Often, the dog will stop and stare at whatever is bothering him, seeming to grow in height as he registers the potential threat.

It is after some or all of these signals have been displayed without the trigger moving away that the stereotypical reactive behaviour will occur. This is the point at which the dog feels they have no other option but overt threats in a last-ditch attempt to drive the trigger away and so we see the classic lunging and barking that is most recognisable as the reactive dog.

Canine body language is at times subtle and can easily be missed by those that have not learned how to read it. Before the point at which the dog launches itself at something or bolts into the distance there will have been a number of signals displayed that may have been missed, causing the dog to escalate to more obvious signs. These signals are categorised into what is known as the 'canine ladder of aggression' devised by Clinical Animal Behaviourist Kendal Shepherd in 2001.

- Biting
- Snapping
- Growling
- Stiffening up, stare
- Lying down, leg up
- Standing crouched, tail tucked under
- Creeping, ears back
- Walking away
- Turning body away, sitting, pawing

- Turning head away
- Yawning, blinking, nose licking

The intensity of the situation increases as the ladder is ascended from yawning upwards, biting being the final resort. Reading this ladder from bottom to top shows how body language escalates as the dog goes from being slightly uncomfortable to having no other recourse in his mind than to bite. In general, most dogs will more or less follow this pattern of escalation, although if their signals have been ignored or, worse, punished in the past, steps may be skipped as the dog moves rapidly to the actions that work to assure his safety. There is a very good reason for the saying 'don't punish the growl' – a growl is communication, no more or less than that. Growling is the dog's only way to tell us that if the frightening situation is not resolved, they will have to move to snapping or biting. While those two steps may not seem much different – I have heard a number of people say that their dog tried to bite them but they moved out of the way in time to avoid the bite – there is a difference. Dogs' reaction times are far faster than human ones. If a dog really wanted to bite a person, they would. Snapping (sometimes called air snapping) near to something or someone is the very last warning that a bite is imminent unless the situation changes rapidly.

Now that we have some idea of what to look for, why do dogs behave in this way? What causes them to react so strongly?

4 WHAT DOES REACTIVITY DO TO THE DOG?

As has been mentioned before, reactivity in dogs is driven by fear.

Fear is a basic, unconscious response to stimuli that may indicate a threat or danger to life or body. In the right context, fear is a vital, life-saving mechanism. Fear triggers a multitude of chemical and physical responses, all of which are geared towards safety and survival. In the right situation, short-term fear can be a literal lifesaver, preparing the body to run away from the danger or fight a way out of the situation. Fear is essential to the survival of wild animals, throughout their evolution and into the present day. The domestic dog, living in our homes, sleeping on our sofas and beds and giving us liberal bursts of 'puppy dog eyes' to persuade us to share the biscuits, is no longer a wild animal. Thousands of years of development to live alongside humans have given us dogs that enjoy our company and the creature comforts that the human home can bring. This evolution has not, however, removed the basic biological drive to survive.

Those of us with phobias can attest to the fact that

fear can be an overwhelming, paralysing entity. It can remove all rational thought, even in a species that is capable of high-level reasoning. Dogs do not reason in the same way that we do and so they have to rely on their instincts. In the case of reactivity, these instincts lead the dog to believe that they are in imminent, severe danger and must be prepared to do whatever it takes to survive the situation.

Some people maintain that dogs do not feel emotions, certainly not in the way that people do, and that to maintain that they do is anthropomorphism of the highest order. Some also claim that dogs do not think in the way that we as humans understand it, that they merely react to situations and stimuli in an instinctive manner, designed purely to survive. Anyone that spends any amount of time with dogs and takes the trouble to actually observe them without any preconceived ideas can see however that dogs do think, if maybe not in the same way as we humans do. A number of studies have also shown that this is not the case, that dogs do think, and do experience emotions.

Gregory Berns set out to discover how dogs' minds work in an ambitious scientific undertaking known as 'The Dog Project.' Using positive reinforcement methods, a number of dogs have been trained to stay in place in a working MRI machine so that functional MRIs (fMRI) could be used to see how the dog's brain responded to stimuli. Not only have these studies answered a number of questions about the canine brain – including the fact that for many dogs, praise is just as rewarding as food, contradicting one frequent negative comment towards positive reinforcement training, that the dog is only ever after the food – but also represent a massive success in their own right for positive reinforcement training. MRI machines are noisy and the dogs are trained to wear ear protection. To remain still for the length of time required for an MRI in such an alien atmosphere shows a remarkable training effort, and just how resilient dogs are capable of being. On a day when I am struggling to get through a situation with my reactive dog, this may seem a little tough to contemplate, but it also inspires me to work harder to make life easier for my boy.

In order to better empathise with and be able to help our fearful, reactive dogs cope with the world, we need to understand further how fear affects the dog. To do this we must take a look at how the fear response system works.

Fear is dealt with by the autonomic nervous system. This is part of the peripheral nervous system – the network of nerves that branch out through the body. Signals are passed from these nerves to the central nervous system, which consists of the brain and spinal cord, and are then analysed, interpreted and assessed as required before instructions on how to deal with whatever created the signal are sent back out through the peripheral nervous system for action to take place. The word autonomous is defined as self-governing or independent. The autonomic nervous system is independent from the conscious control of the dog. It deals with the involuntary processes that take place in the body – keeping the lungs working in the cycle of respiration, keeping the heart beating etc. Fear is also involuntary, out of the dog's control.

The autonomic nervous system splits into two more systems. The parasympathetic nervous system (PNS) is responsible for what is known as the 'rest and digest' system, the functions of the body when everything is normal and fine. Fear is the domain of the other part, the sympathetic nervous system (SNS). All of these different parts being called nervous systems is a little confusing, but everything linked to the fear response is neatly contained in the sympathetic system. The term 'fight or flight' is well known, and this is the response the sympathetic nervous system deals with.

When a situation is perceived as being stressful, such as a dog encountering one of his triggers, the response begins in the brain with the amygdala tripping the hypothalamus into action. Signals are sent to the pituitary gland, also in the brain, which produces a hormone called ACTH. This, together with a signal from the hypothalamus, heads to the adrenal glands located on the kidneys, which release adrenaline. Chemical messengers in the blood also prompt the adrenal cortex to produce cortisol. The result of these chemicals is a body that is prepared to run away or fight to defend itself if required.

A number of changes occur in the body during this process. The liver provides glucose into the bloodstream as an extra energy source if running away becomes necessary. Changes take place in the circulatory system, with increased blood pressure, an increased heart rate and stronger, more forceful heart muscle contractions. The pupils of the eyes dilate. Constriction of the blood vessels supplying the urinary and gastrointestinal tracts decreases blood flow to these systems, slowing urine production and digestive activity. Energy that is usually directed to the immune system is redirected to preparing for 'fight or flight' to maximise the amount available to survive the imminent encounter. Increased breathing capacity via dilated bronchioles increases oxygen intake to facilitate running away, and breathing is faster. All of these changes are part of the instinctive survival response.

Adrenaline produced in the body during the fear response can clear the body rapidly, within fifteen minutes of the trigger being gone. Cortisol may take much longer to leave the system, from forty-eight hours to as many as six days according to some studies, dependent on how strong the reaction to the trigger was. Once the stress hormones have dissipated, the PNS comes into effect to restore homeostasis in the body, returning to the dog's baseline normal and the 'rest or digest' state.

Although we refer mainly to the 'fight or flight' response to fear and stress, there are a number of potential reactions to stress, known as the 'Fs'. The list also includes freeze, faint and fool around.

Freeze means doing absolutely nothing, with the dog remaining completely still and hoping the problem does not see them and goes away. This gives the dog time without taking an action to assess the situation while not provoking a response from the trigger. The dog that is in a freeze will not take food or respond to any cues or commands from the handler.

Fainting due to severe fear can happen in dogs just as it can in people, although in these cases it is almost certain that there is a pre-existing medical condition.

Fooling around can also be known as fidgeting because the dog absolutely cannot sit still. It is a form of coping mechanism, a frantic kind of response in a stressful situation such as at the vets. The dog will show really overt, over the top play behaviours like biting and ragging the lead, rolling around, play bowing and jumping up. It is a displacement type behaviour – a normal canine behaviour being shown at an unusual, inappropriate time in an attempt to shift the focus from one situation to another.

Flight does not mean simply running away, although that is a valid way to escape from a stressful situation. Flight includes any kind of behaviour in which the dog tries to make distance between themselves and the trigger. This can include not only running, but also hiding behind their handler or attempting to climb up them to gain height away from the trigger.

Fight is the final option, when the dog feels there is no other option to get safely out of the situation than to fight it out. This is when the aggressive displays are seen, moving up the ladder of aggression until either they find something that works or are forced to fight.

Recent studies have shown another 'F' – fornicate. Obviously, that is a slightly different kind of stress and a definite focus shift! Not all stress is negatively based, although the stress involved in reactivity is.

This is what happens when the dog is scared. In the short term, fear is a natural, healthy part of life and the dog will soon recover, once homeostasis has been re-established and the dog returned to their baseline normal biological state. What if this return to normal does not get to happen, and the dog does not get to ever really relax?

As has been mentioned before, cortisol can take some time to leave the body. If, due to chronic stress in the dog, cortisol levels are not able to drop to normal levels, we can start to see a number of issues arising in and for our dogs, both from a health and behavioural perspective. From a biological perspective, the fear response is designed to be a short-term thing, a survival mechanism aimed at getting the animal out of a situation alive. It is not designed to be running at high alert permanently, but this is what can be happening in a reactive dog.

As humans, we know how stress can make us feel if it goes on for a long time. It is, to put it mildly, an unpleasant feeling. Dogs experience the same symptoms, without the ability to analyse and understand the situation in the same way that humans can.

The stress response diverts blood flow and energy away from the bodily systems that are regarded as not essential for immediate survival. This includes the digestive system – one of the signs that will tell you that your dog is extremely stressed by a situation is that they will refuse to take food or treats, no matter how much you offer their favourites. When preparing to run from a dangerous situation, the last thing an animal will need is a full stomach. Urine production will also slow, as a running dog will not want to have to stop to toilet. The immune system is also regarded as non-essential to survive an imminent encounter. This makes sense from a short-term perspective, but it is not difficult to see why a suppressed immune system long-term can only lead to trouble.

The combination of not eating properly and feeling sick at a constant low level will leave the reactive dog feeling lethargic and tired. They will likely try to sleep more. Elevated stress levels make sleep more elusive however, compounding the problem yet further. A fearful dog will also be hyper vigilant, trying to keep watch all around their surroundings to ensure the things they are scared of cannot creep up on them unawares, and will find it very hard to 'switch off' and relax. The less the dog wants to eat and the less they sleep, the worse they will feel and so the problem enters a vicious cycle.

The constant stress affects the dog's stomach, and they may present with diarrhoea. A previously house-trained dog may start to toilet inappropriately inside the house. If going outside on a walk has become a scary experience, the dog is not going to feel comfortable putting themselves in the vulnerable position required for toileting outside and will instead possibly find a spot inside their safe haven instead. Of course, this can then lead to further stress if the poor dog's guardian does not understand and chastises or, even worse, punishes the dog on finding the mess. All this will lead to however is that the dog will hide their indoor toileting spot better. Shouting at or chastising a dog is never the answer, particularly a fearful dog who, by their very nature, is a particularly sensitive creature. In this situation, all the guardian would succeed in doing is teaching the dog that it is also not safe to toilet where their human will find it.

Dry, itchy skin may be seen, with the dog developing dandruff or being seen constantly scratching and biting himself. If the root cause if not addressed, this can become habitual as a form of coping mechanism, and can lead to the poor dog making himself extremely uncomfortable and sore, therefore increasing stress levels and making the problem even worse.

As in humans, constantly elevated stress levels can be detrimental to the dog's mental health. As is obvious given that we are looking specifically at fearful dogs, our dogs can suffer from anxiety. Worse, they can also suffer from depression. Chronic stress will make these feelings worse.

If the reactive dog is not allowed to ever recover fully from stress, his body systems start to find ways to 'cope' under the cortisol load, to adapt to it. This is not a good thing, as it leads to adaptation diseases. These can include problems with the kidneys and cardiovascular disease, including heart disease, high blood pressure and abnormal heart rhythms. All of these can make your dog feel more ill and vulnerable, therefore adding to the stress. Unchecked, these issues can lead to the worst possible outcome of all, the death of the dog.

Having looked at what reactivity does to the dog, both physically and mentally, it is easy to see why it is necessary to find a way to help make them feel better about the world and to be able to deal with it on an emotional level. The terminology often used (and I am guilty of this myself at times) is to teach the dog to 'cope' with the world, but the aim should be to reach far higher than this, and allow the dog to learn that the world can be an enjoyable, rewarding place. We shall look later at ways to put this into action.

5 WHAT DOES REACTIVITY DO TO THE OWNER?

This question is at the heart of the inspiration for this book. Owning and living with a reactive dog can be an incredibly difficult, lonely experience. Until you have lived with – or at least walked with – a fearful, reactive dog, it is not something that you can really understand. Having a pet is meant to be an enjoyable, enriching experience. Having a dog is supposed to, in most people's minds, lead to nice walks in lovely places, or at least the enjoyment of watching your dog running, romping and playing amongst friends both human and canine. The perfect mental picture of owning a dog does not include walking at times of the day when all sensible people are tucked up in bed, especially in the dark and cold of winter, or running to get the dog out for a walk because it has started pouring with rain and that means most people with dogs will be inside in the warm and dry. For some of us, however, that is the reality.

There are a number of different emotions that may crop up at certain times in your journey with your fearful dog, frequently several in quick succession on particularly difficult days.

Shock

The first feeling recognisably linked to living with a reactive dog is often shock. A fearful dog in full reaction mode is indeed a shocking sight, and it can be very hard to reconcile the growling, snarling ball of hair in front of you with the much-loved family member that curls up next to you on the sofa. This is particularly true the first time a full-blown reaction takes place. Certainly, in my own case, I had never witnessed anything like what I saw my dog do, and at that time I knew nothing about reactivity or the signs that I had missed for my dog to reach that point. Once you and your dog are safely away from the trigger that caused the overt reactivity it is important to be kind to you both, you and your dog, as the pair of you will have been through a difficult experience from which you will require time to recover.

Embarrassment / Humiliation

Any that have been in a position of their dog reacting to another dog being walked by those that do not understand fearful dogs exist will know 'the look' that you're subjected to. The one that seems to be designed to shame you for bringing your 'aggressive, dangerous' dog out in public. The very first time my own fearful dog reacted was when we were approaching the end of a bridlepath, and an older couple were walking their dogs along the pavement at a right angle to us. My young dog reacted to the man walking the first of these dogs, and the expression on his face as he stopped and stared at me is one that will stay with me forever. His wife with the second dog behind was much more understanding and spoke to her dog saying 'No, he doesn't want to say hello,' as her dog moved towards mine and kept him walking past. I heard the man say 'That dog shouldn't be out in public,' and that finished me off. I had to hand the lead over to my husband who was walking with us, and spent the rest of the walk home in tears.

That is something that just has to be accepted when you realise you have a reactive dog. There is a very high probability that you will spend time in tears. I have cried more over one dog (who is young and in perfect health) than over any of my others, even those I have lost. Most of the people I have ever spoken to, either face-to-face or online, say that they have cried due to their reactive dog. The chances are it will happen. This is nothing to be embarrassed about. Living with a fearful dog is a difficult experience, even for those far more experienced with dogs than the average pet owner (yes, professional dog trainers, coaches and behaviourists can experience the same issues with reactive dogs as the rest of us, although they are better equipped in the beginning to be able to start improving the situation). Let it out and move on.

Anger

There can be a knee-jerk reaction even if the fear aggressive display is directed towards someone or something else, for the owner who has never encountered reactivity before, and not yet found the facilities to learn and understand what reactivity is and does, to take their dog's behaviour as some kind of personal affront and become angry with them. This holds even more true if the stressed dog has redirected some of their fear and turned on the handler or a companion dog. Redirection is as unconscious as everything else surrounding reactivity. The dog is so scared and desperate to escape that they attack the first thing that they come to. There is no personal element to it at all, although being bitten by your dog, or seeing one of your dogs attacking a housemate is obviously an upsetting experience. Anger is one of the most destructive emotions in any situation, let alone one involving fear. If you feel yourself becoming angry at your dog, create some distance so that you can cool off and re-establish your emotional balance. That can mean cutting short a walk and heading home so everyone can chill and relax, or giving your dog something to chew or exercise their brain so that you can have a rest from interacting while the resentment does down. Many people with reactive dogs will have had these moments and these feelings and it is a natural response in the heat of the moment, feeling that your dog's 'bad' behaviour is ruining your time together that should be fun and enjoyable. This is the time to remind yourself of one very important truth – your dog is not behaving like this to annoy you. Your dog is not giving you a hard time, your dog is having a hard time. Remembering this fact goes a long way to helping cope with anger when it arises.

Loneliness

The journey with a reactive dog, at least in the very beginning, is without doubt a lonely one. Just how lonely depends on a number of factors, not least the extent of your dog's reactivity and to what they are actually reactive. A dog that reacts to tall men with beards wearing hats is going to have an easier time than one that is stressed by any other dog or person. In personal experience, we have to deal with a dog scared of all strangers and all unknown dogs, so our path is a particularly lonely one that involves very unsociable hours to have peaceful walks. Fortunately, the dog in question in this household is not bothered by walking in the dark, and the person walking him is no longer worried about the dark either! No matter the level of reactivity in your dog though, at some point you are likely to feel alone in the world, just you and your dog. Whether it is the people around you not understanding what you are going through, or the isolation of having to stay away from anyone and everyone to avoid triggering your dog's reactions, there will be some extent of loneliness.

Nerves

This is a feeling that will be easily recognisable to anyone with a fearful furry friend. That trepidation that comes when you are gearing up and about to set foot outside of the door. Will you manage to get around your chosen walk without problems? Will you even be able to get to the end of the street without incident? Have you timed it right so that the people with the big bouncy dog with no recall will not be out as well? It becomes an inconvenient and unpleasant truth that no walk ever starts without worries, and it is very difficult not to let those nerves reach the dog. Remember, you are physically connected by a lead when walking, and your dog can sense every one of your emotions. If you go out convinced it is all going to go horribly wrong, there is an increased chance that it will.

Exhaustion

Being constantly on alert and worrying that your dog is going to react to something is beyond tiring. That hour a day or however long you walk your particular dog is a very long time to be constantly scanning the visible horizon in all directions and mentally dreading seeing anyone or anything. It is likely that you will experience the feeling of returning home after an outing physically, mentally and (particularly) emotionally drained. This is incredibly wearing and hard to live with.

Despair

Everything mentioned above can all roll together to leave the guardian of a reactive dog feeling utterly despondent. Many might feel that there is no solution, and that they have to do something drastic such as rehoming what is still a much-loved pet, as they see no other way out of the situation. It is a fact that very few people that have travelled this road will not have had the rehoming thoughts at some point, or solutions that are even more drastic. It is sadly easy to become stuck in a train of thought that there is nothing that can be done to improve the situation and give all concerned a happier life together. Fortunately, there are options that will be examined later, so this stage need not be given into in a hurry.

There is one important thing to remember when considering your own feelings regarding reactivity. So far most of what has been described is how stress affects the dog. Humans are mammals too, and the stress responses work exactly the same way in us as in our canine companions. We have the same stress hormones in us as dogs do, and they are stimulated and produced in the same way. Long term stress will have exactly the same detrimental effects on us as it will our dogs, leading to problems with physical and mental health. Human beings have a much higher capacity for analysing and reasoning through a situation. After all, the most intelligent dog is working at a similar level to a human toddler, and it is to be hoped that anyone in charge of a dog is rather older and more mature than a toddler. However, reasoning and analysis can take time to kick in, and our initial emotional response is likely to be similar to that of our dogs, simply shorter in duration and less visibly demonstrated due to the differences in the way we view the world and communicate with it.

This is where the phrase 'be kind to yourself' can come in very useful. It is all very well and good ensuring that we deal with the stresses and linked problems for our dogs, but this will not be able to take full effect unless we address the same problems in ourselves. Nothing good ever comes from listening to the incredibly destructive phrases like 'Man up!' or belittling the emotional effect of a difficult day with our dogs. That is something to be wary of if surrounded by people that do not know or understand the difficulties and restrictions that we live with. Any form of suppressing valid emotions will only ever lead to the problem being made much worse in the long term.

It is vital that we, the guardians or handlers of these fearful dogs, let ourselves own the emotions that we experience during the bad times with our dogs. Only by admitting them to ourselves and allowing them to run their course can we accept them and let them go. This is an important point. When taking our fearful dogs out and about, we need to be utterly clear of negative emotions. Dogs are such incredibly sensitive creatures that they know how we are feeling at any time. How many times have you felt a bit down, and had your dog come and sit quietly with you, maybe offering a comforting paw or leaning against your leg? There is no faking of emotional responses when it comes to dogs. Unlike when interacting with other humans, we cannot simply paste on a fake smile and fool them. Given how sensitive dogs are, and how good they are at sensing emotions, there is no doubt that our dogs are going to know that we are stressed. This can turn into a vicious cycle - dogs and handlers that go out in a state of stress are going to be almost looking for problems, which hugely increases the chances of encountering one. Make sure that you have dealt with all of the negativity you might be feeling, so that you can head out with positivity and give your dog (and yourself) the best experience that you can manage in the available conditions.

A quick note on rehoming: this book is concentrating on the idea of working to improve the relationships and life for the fearful dog to be able to remain in his home with his guardians. There will doubtless be occasions when the guardian feels that, for whatever reason, they can no longer cope with the dog's difficulties and surrender them to a rescue. So long as the dog's well-being is safeguarded and they go to a responsible rescue, fosterer or new guardian, this is not a decision to be demonised. Living with a reactive dog is not easy by any means, and is not what the vast majority of dog guardians signed up for when bringing a furry family member into their homes. Changing the behaviour and mentality behind the reactivity is not a quick or easy process, and not something that every dog guardian will be able to follow through on without the emotional turbulence affecting them. Many that surrender their dogs in these circumstances feel bitter disappointment and grief at having to give up on their dog, but that they had no other choice. Again, so long as the dog is safe and well cared for that decision could be the best for all concerned, rather than both parties feeling worse as the problems intensify. If the guardian is unable to follow a behaviour modification programme that helps the dog there will be no improvement, and quite possibly the problem will become greater. In these cases, the guardian that realises this early on and rehomes the dog to a person or rescue that will be able to help the dog can only be praised for having the self-awareness and lack of ego to put the dog's welfare above all else. It has to be stressed that the right rescue, rehoming centre or new home must be carefully researched and located. A good rescue will pair the reactive dog with a fosterer or new home that will be well placed to help the dog feel more secure with life.

Hope?

This chapter and the one before it may have painted a dark picture of what happens within and outside of the reactive dog, and inside the guardian or handler. There is hope, however. There are ways of working to improve the mental situation of both dog and guardian and to remove at least some of the stress that is involved in sharing the same space together and with others. It is unfortunately not possible to promise that everything will be fine. All dogs are completely individual, as are their guardians, and this includes everything to do with their reactivity. With some exceptions, following the right advice, finding the right support and methods of working with the fearful dog, things can often be distinctly improved.

6 THE IMPORTANCE OF SUPPORT

As discussed in previous chapters, the life of the newly-discovered reactive dog owner can be a lonely one. Having a dog that cannot tolerate being near other dogs, or people, or whatever else your dog might be fearful of, is obviously isolating by its very nature. Unfortunately, the temptation in the beginning can be to isolate yourself further voluntarily by avoiding all contact with others. Yes, avoiding encounters with triggers is a part of the process, but a vital part of surviving with your sanity intact is finding some appropriate support.

Support is a multi-pronged addition for the dog guardian. Many seek out support early on, with the use of trainers or puppy classes when they have young puppies, or for when a new adult dog has joined the family as a rescue or through other rehoming. This is practical support, offering advice and guidance on how to ensure that you and your dog have a happy, relaxed life together. Through classes, or via social walks or just meeting other people on walks, dog guardians can build up a network of friends and acquaintances that have dogs, and form a social support network.

One important point before going any further: if, on

reflection, no warning signs of the dog being scared have been observed before the onset of reactivity, it is important that a vet carries out a full physical examination. This is probably a good idea in any case of reactivity beginning, to rule out any health problems that might be contributing to the behavioural change. A number of conditions can cause a dog to show a change in behaviour. Some illnesses can cause a disturbance in hormone levels, which will affect the way the dog feels in himself. Another factor which can definitely alter behaviour is if the dog is in pain. Any level of pain is likely to make a dog feel vulnerable and may make them prone to lashing out. Dogs are by nature generally very stoic (although as in everything, they are all individuals and some are very definitely not stoic at all!), as are many predator animals. From an evolutionary perspective, it makes little sense in most cases for animals to obviously display anything that will hamper their chances of survival, so they will frequently keep their pain signals very much minimised. If in any doubt at all, a visit to the vet for a complete clinical examination and possible blood tests could rule out any health-related issues and mean that you can rule those out as potential causes for behaviour change.

As discussed in the previous two chapters, reactive behaviour is both the sign of and the cause of huge amounts of stress in both dog and guardian. Both halves of the partnership need support to be able to cope with these stresses. But while the owner or handler can provide some measure of support to the fearful dog as soon as the difficulties are recognised, who is supporting the owner?

A session with an online search engine for sources of practical support can soon have a worried owner finding articles and websites offering advice on how to 'fix' your reactive dog. As with everything else on the internet, the quality of advice varies wildly. There are many trainers and behaviourists that can be found on the internet, either via search engine and visiting their websites, or via social media (in particular Facebook) who will offer advice. There are many excellent trainers with many years of experience that will do this, but there are also some utter charlatans. Before taking the advice of someone claiming to be a professional, be sure to check them out thoroughly. If you have taken your dog to your vet's surgery to be checked over, they may be able to recommend a behaviourist that they work with regularly, or give you a referral to one. It is still important to check them out and be sure that you would be happy with them coming to consult about your dog. Always remember that this is your dog at the centre of this, and you are well within your rights to ensure that anyone involved in his care and wellbeing in any form has his welfare at the absolute centre of their priorities.

It may be that, for a variety of reasons, a fearful dog's guardian decides that it would be better for their dog's mental and emotional health for them to work on their dog's reactivity themselves. Often this is the case for guardians whose dogs are scared of people outside the circle of their known and safe family and friends. This is the situation with my own fearful dog, who has a very small trusted circle consisting of family members. To put him through the stress and fear of having to meet a strange person, especially if they were to come into his home, would be hugely detrimental to his mental well-being. As much as I want to work on the difficulties that we have with his reactivity, forcing him to see a stranger in his own home would cause him far too much upset for me to contemplate. There are professionals that offer help via video calling sessions, which may suit some people as a compromise at the beginning to help them get started with a behaviour modification programme while keeping stress levels at a minimum for the people reactive dog. Trainers will be discussed in more detail in a later chapter.

Practical support for the dog guardian who chooses to go it alone and work on improving their dogs' thresholds and confidence levels themselves can be found online and in a number of books. Trainers' websites can also be a good source of articles and resources that can help, and some offer free email courses which are worth exploring to broaden your knowledge of the subject of reactivity, both in terms of how and why dogs display reactive behaviour, and how to work with them to change their outlook on the things that scare them. A look on a popular search engine for 'reactivity in dogs' brings up a number of links to articles written by well-regarded trainers and behaviourists. Popular and well-known does not, of course, always mean good. After all, one of the best-known trainers in the world has no training in canine coaching or behaviour, and promotes methods which show no regard for the mental or emotional well-being of the dog. Read articles in links carefully until you have the measure of the author. At the first sight of any of the words, dominance, correction, alpha or pack leader, shut the book, close down that web page and go back to a fresh search. In a very short period of time, you will be able to pick up very quickly whether the writer of the article is working from a scientifically valid viewpoint, or still sticks to the old-fashioned flawed theory.

Once you have been able to identify a core group of expert trainers and behaviourists, who are clearly working from a scientifically based positive perspective, then you will have a good library of helpful advice to be able to access. While many behaviourists and trainers will have published books that you can buy (and some of these may well be worth investing in), they will frequently have excellent excerpts and other behaviour articles on their websites that can be accessed free of charge. These can help provide the beginnings of answers on how to help your fearful dog, and can aid you in deciding if the authors' style of writing and advice makes them worth investing in copies of their books.

There are a number of books concerning reactive

dogs that come highly recommended to help gain an understanding of what goes on in the mind of a scared dog, how they communicate that fear through body language, and how to begin to help them. I have highlighted a few here that I have found particularly helpful, especially in the more novice stages of working with my own fearful dog, or that have come highly recommended by a number of well-known, qualified and experienced trainers and behaviourists.

Inspiring Resilience in Fearful and Reactive Dogs by Sally Gutteridge. Sally is a fantastic writer with an excellent ability to explain the science behind concepts while avoiding confusing the issue with technical jargon, making her advice accessible to everyone, no matter how much or little they have studied dog behaviour to this point.

Don't Shoot the Dog by Karen Pryor. Originally published some time ago now, there is reference in this book to some morally dubious practices in animal training and husbandry in the past, but that should not be allowed to put anyone off reading, as the text came in part from less enlightened times regarding animal welfare. While at first glance, it may seem that the use of the word 'dog' in the title is misleading as some of the information inside regards training other species, the concept of the training is valid for just about any species.

Canine Behaviour: A Photo Illustrated Handbook by Barbara Handelman. Although not cheap, this comes high on the recommended list. The photographs are beautifully clear and perfectly demonstrate the canine body language. The text explanations are wonderfully descriptive and explain clearly what is going on in the photos.

On Talking Terms With Dogs: Calming Signals by Turid Rugaas. This book contains excellent descriptions and photographs describing the signals that dogs use, and I would recommend every dog guardian reads it to gain a greater understanding of what their dog is telling them.

Fight!: A Practical Guide to the Treatment of Dog - Dog Aggression by Jean Donaldson. While there are one or two things in this book that I do not like (the section on putting on a headcollar and ignoring the dog's efforts to remove it in particular) this book is useful in giving a step by step guide to a method of improving reactivity to other dogs.

Feisty Fido - Help for the Leash Reactive Dog by Patricia McConnell and Karen London. This is a short book compared to most, but that simply makes it a handy pocket size! Again, it provides a step-by-step guide to help improve on-lead walks for you and your lead reactive dog.

Click to Calm: Healing the Aggressive Dog by Emma Parsons. If nothing else from this book, I recommend reading the introduction to get the perfect explanation of why forceful, punishment-based training using aversive gadgets is the worst thing you can do for a fearful dog (I do actually recommend reading far more than the introduction, obviously!) and how it can make matters much worse.

BAT 2.0 by Grisha Stewart. BAT stands for Behaviour Adjustment Training, and is a method devised by this book's author. BAT will be explored a little further in a later chapter.

As important as practical support is for the reactive dog guardian, emotional support is also necessary. In fact, it may well be more important for the human involved than practical support. As discussed before, reactivity is not just hard on the dog but on the guardian or handler as well. All of the negative emotions identified as being experienced by the guardian when a walk has gone badly. When trigger stacking has meant that the day seems to have been filled by one explosion after another as it has just been impossible for the fearful dog to find the space and peace that he needs to calm down. All of these things can combine to cause serious mental and emotional trauma to the dog's guardian.

While this portion of the chapter is far shorter than the practical support section it is the emotional support or lack of it that can make or break the success of any behaviour adjustment attempts, or even the long-term future of the reactive dog in that particular home.

One of the most useful effects finding emotional support has is removing that feeling of isolation and loneliness. Finding local support can be difficult as so often other dog guardians and walkers in the area have never had to deal with a reactive dog themselves, and may well view them as purely aggressive rather than scared. This will not lead to a supportive relationship.

Social media is a channel that may have many shortcomings, but for the reactive dog guardian, it can be a lifeline. There is a reactive dogs community on Reddit, and a large number of groups can be found on Facebook by searching the term reactive dogs. As with any online resource care must be exercised when deciding which of these to join, but most groups will contain at least some useful guidance and supportive members. As always, it is worth taking the time to thoroughly read all of the guidance to ensure that the group is working from positive, force free and scientifically valid viewpoints.

In these groups is where the largest concentration of those people that understand will be found. Those people that really get it, what it is like to be the person on the other end of the lead from a furious ball of hackles and teeth. Finding the right group like this can be a lifeline to maintaining your mental health. The right group when you find it is a place where you can talk about the things that have gone wrong and feel nothing but empathy and understanding, and get advice to help you calm your dog and yourself.

It is not being over dramatic to say that at times, this

support is what could preserve a reactive dog guardian's sanity.

7 RIGHT TYPE OF TRAINER

To begin the process of finding the right way to help you and your dog, the first thing to look at is how dogs actually learn. What actually is training? The answer is relatively simple. Training in animals is behaviour manipulation. We take behaviours that the animal offers, in the beginning utterly natural behaviours, and manipulate the situation so that it is in their interests to offer the behaviours that we want. The methods that we use to ensure that those desirable behaviours are repeated will fall into one of four categories: positive punishment, negative reinforcement, negative punishment and positive reinforcement. These are what are known as the four quadrants of operant conditioning in training jargon. There is a long and involved explanation of what operant conditioning is, with mention of Pavlov and Skinner, but to cut a long story short, it relies on the principle that actions have consequences and these consequences can be good or bad. Good consequences make a dog more likely to repeat a behaviour, bad consequences make repetition less likely. The words 'positive' and 'negative' in the titles of these quadrants do not mean good and bad, but are used in the scientific sense, in that something is added to a situation or is taken away from a situation.

A brief summary of the four quadrants from the least humane, useful and constructive to the ones that will get results in a force free manner:

Positive punishment: something bad happens after an undesired behaviour, such as a 'correction' (jerk on the lead), being shouted at or kicked, a shock from a shock collar or being hit. All of these result in added pain and fear for the dog. While ensuring that the behaviour is less likely to be repeated, they are morally repugnant as they rely on causing a sentient animal to experience pain and distress. The technical term for something the dog does not like is an 'aversive stimulus' and these are often obvious. Anything that causes pain or fear is clearly aversive. It goes further than that as anything that the dog does not like and will try to avoid is aversive.

Negative reinforcement: something bad is taken away when a desirable behaviour happens, such as a lead being relaxed so that the prong collar stops digging in when teaching loose lead walking. This relies on the dog being caused pain for a length of time in a training session so that it can be taken away when the dog gets it right. Again, a sentient creature is caused pain and distress to alter their natural behaviour.

Negative punishment: something good is taken away when an undesirable behaviour occurs. A toy, a play session, something that the dog enjoys is denied him. This is not ideal but, used sparingly and with close attention to the timing of the removal, it can play a part in a force free programme.

Positive reinforcement: this is by far the best of the four quadrants from the dog's perspective. Desired behaviour is rewarded by something the dog really likes. That may be food, attention, a favourite toy or play session. The individual dog decides what the rewards should be, and the order of value of rewards he finds more enticing, which should be used for more difficult tasks or environments. It is more enjoyable for the person doing the training as well, as dogs trained using positive reinforcement are likely to enjoy their training sessions and take part enthusiastically. A happy, enthusiastic student makes a rewarding training environment.

That is the science of how dogs learn. It is the basis of every part of training, and of behaviour modification. The next step is to decide how exactly that science is going to be utilised. There are two basic options available to the fearful dog guardian. They can either go it alone, following a behaviour modification programme that they have found and feel that they can make work for them and their dog or they can find a trainer or behaviourist to help them implement one.

Broadly speaking, trainers can be divided into a number of rough categories:

1. Punishment and dominance-based trainers
2. 'Balanced' trainers
3. LIMA trainers
4. Positive trainers

The problem with using the dominance theory when it comes to training dogs has been discussed in a previous chapter. Even if there was any validity in the concept of dogs vying for dominance in the way that theory espouses (and they really do not), that still does not really make sense of why dogs would be attempting dominance over humans in their household. We and our dogs are not a 'pack' in that sense and, while some people do treat their dogs like little humans, our dogs are definitely smart enough not to think of us as big, strange looking dogs! Using the so-called 'alpha roll' on your dog is not going to 'put him in his place' or establish you as the pack leader. At best your dog will probably wonder what on earth you are doing, and there is a good chance that you could scare him and make him lose confidence and trust in you. When working with a fearful dog that is the very last thing you want to have happen. Everything that you do should be done with the aim of reinforcing and strengthening the bond with your dog, and increasing that level of trust and confidence. A dog that feels he can rely on you to keep him safe is going to be that little bit more responsive to behaviour modification, counter conditioning and desensitisation, whichever method is used and works well for both handler and dog.

Any use of positive punishment will also result in a damaged relationship between handler and dog. Imagine if you were in a situation that you found confusing, strange and scary. You cannot speak to communicate that fact and so you let the person that you trust to look after you know in the only way you can. Instead of comforting and protecting you, they yank on the lead, hurting your neck, or shout at you confusing and scaring you further or, even worse, they hit you. None of these will make you any less scared or confused. In fact, they will only make you worse, and possibly feel like you have to defend yourself. We already know that reactive dogs behave as they do because it is their way of creating distance and trying to keep themselves safe, so it does not take any imagination to realise how they do that. Most dogs are far more forgiving than people that use positive punishment deserve however, and the result is more likely to be a cringing dog that displays even more fearful body language in response to the handler.

A reactive, fearful dog is already living in a state of stress and fear. How can anything that causes more fear and pain possibly be a good way of dealing with that? Simply put, it cannot. At best, the poor dog now feels as if he has to be wary of his handlers. At worst, he may begin to feel that he has to defend himself against the people hurting and scaring him, and start to become reactive towards his guardians and family members. In either case, this is making life worse for the dog, and could have serious repercussions for his mental health, possibly even his life.

Trainers that refer to themselves as balanced try to sell that phrase as being a positive one. Balance in all things is surely good, after all. In terms of working with dogs however, it is not a positive thing. Yes, they will use elements of positive reinforcement but also rely heavily on equipment based in the much less desirable quadrants such as shock and prong collars, or other 'lesser' aversive measures such as bottles filled with stones to throw down and make a noise to interrupt undesirable behaviours. While the positive reinforcement side to what they do is good, there is still the strong likelihood that they will use, or will cause you to use methods on your dog that will scare and hurt them.

The category that exists between the balanced trainers and the entirely positive, force free, uses what these trainers call LIMA, 'Least Intrusive, Minimally Aversive' methods. These trainers largely use positive techniques and, while the use of aversive measures is not entirely ruled out, they will be minimised. Although the progression of science and the understanding of how dogs learn mean that truly positive trainers are becoming more common and easier to find, the old-fashioned methods are still widely found. In the absence of being able to contact a truly positive, force free professional to help with your fearful dog, LIMA is the best option if you feel unable to cope with the situation alone. It may be a good idea to ask some questions to gauge what the trainer regards as minimally aversive, to ensure that they will not use any methods that you find morally unsupportable, and which you feel would cause any harm to your dog.

Finally, we come to the positive trainers. These are rooted firmly in the positive reinforcement quadrant of learning, with occasional very careful usage of negative punishment, but practised only when there is no positive reinforcement solution for that particular situation, used only sparingly and utilising very careful timing to ensure that the negative punishment marks the right behaviour. Ideally, the positive trainer will then switch up the session for the dog to succeed at something, often by switching the cue and behaviour being cued to something that the dog knows and has performed successfully a number of times before so that he can end the session with a 'win' and be rewarded via positive reinforcement.

Trainers from the dominance based and balanced categories will often denigrate the way in which positive trainers work, usually by claiming that positive reinforcement is 'bribing' the dog to do what we want. Dogs should obey us as we are the masters by their thinking, or because we provide their meals and a place for them to sleep. I look at this another way. When we give a dog a command, or as I prefer to call it a cue, for a particular behaviour, be that a sit, down, roll over or whatever else your dog knows how to do, that is essentially asking them to work, and why should they work for nothing? Once a behaviour is established and the dog is happily doing as requested when cued, then the reward can be phased out, so that it goes from a treat every time the dog sits, to every other time, or on a random numbered repeat so that the dog never knows when he is going to be rewarded. An analogy to explain why this works is the slot machines in casinos. The longer a person sits there pulling the lever without winning anything, the more convinced they become that 'this' time will be the winner, because the payout has to come at some time. This will keep the dog repeating the behaviour, in the hope that this time he will get a treat. Stop them completely and eventually the dog will stop as well. Would you work for absolutely no return? Why should your dog? He is not going to make a connection between training in the early afternoon and dinner that evening. Treats (or attention or fuss if he is not keen on treats) are his wages for doing as we ask, and it's really a pretty good return on investment when he is trained to the level you want.

Positive trainers will also potentially call themselves by the name 'canine coaches' and might use more coaching methods than traditional training methods. Rather than putting the dog in a starting position where he can either get it right or wrong, coaches will often put a dog in a position where he can start offering behaviours that he thinks the human might like, and then reward the behaviour they have been looking for. This allows the dog a greater element of thinking for himself and working out the problem without being guided directly to it. This method of coaching rather than teaching behaviours and cues in a more traditional manner can be very empowering for the dog, and could lead to a more confident, outgoing dog as he comes to realise that he can come up with the answers himself without direct human assistance. He will be more likely to offer behaviours in the future having gained this confidence by being coached rather than taught.

There is one extra warning when searching for a trainer, and this applies to all canine training needs, but especially when it comes to reactive dogs. Training overall will not be a quick thing, it is an ongoing process of gradual improvement and expansion of ideas. Anyone that offers a solution that will have your dog 'better' in a matter of days, or suggests that your dog goes to stay with them for residential training should be definitely rejected as possible trainers for you. Fear and reactivity make for a complicated mental situation, and there is simply no 'fix' that can be guaranteed to work in a short space of time. Residential training is also a bad idea as there is no way of knowing how your dog is being treated while away from home. There is also the fact that, when it comes to handling a fearful dog, the handler needs to feel happy and relaxed on the other end of the lead, and that comes from working through the problem together and making progress. Having your dog come home after a few days away, there is still going to be that trepidation when going out for that first walk. Even if the residential trainer has managed to make some progress, the guardian's nerves on that first walk could easily undo some of that improvement, as they have not seen it for themselves and so may not have confidence that the dog is feeling better about the scary things.

Training methods are a very divisive subject, and a large number of trainers can be extremely vociferous and hold very strong opinions stating that the way they train dogs is the only way to successfully train. I would respectfully suggest that if a professional trainer that you contact ever tells you 'my way is the only way and you must do things exactly my way,' then you should keep on searching. Even when it comes to the positive trainers and coaches. We are in a golden time for the study of dogs and canine psychology, and so the science is constantly evolving as we learn more about the way in which the canine brain works. Positive reinforcement has even been used to train dogs to remain motionless in MRI machines to allow functional MRI scans to be run. If that does not prove the capacity of positive reinforcement as a training ideology, then it is possible nothing ever will!

8 PRACTICAL STEPS TO EMOTIONAL PEACE

As has been said previously, the list of things that a dog can be scared of is extensive, and there may well be more than one thing on any dog's particular list. In the case of my own dog that started my studies on the subject, his list includes dogs, people, noisy vehicles, cars on wet roads and dramatic music on the television!

Different fear causing stimuli can be tackled using different methods. They all come under the heading of 'behaviour modification', which sounds a little scary and like something out of a cold war era dystopian novel. It simply means changing behaviour, and it is the result that we are working for with the reactive dog, to make them more comfortable with the things that scare them and so able to display more relaxed behaviour around these stimuli, rather than feeling the need to display fear aggression and other stress related behaviours.

Before beginning

Trigger stacking is a concept raised in an earlier chapter. It can take days for cortisol to leave the body, and so it stands to reason that trigger stacking can happen over more than one day, not just on a single day. For that reason, one piece of advice often given to aid working with your reactive dog is to start out by giving them a 'cortisol break' – a period of time in which they encounter no triggers. This may mean taking them to a secure field, walking somewhere you know that there is no chance of encountering any of the dog's triggers or not walking at all.

Something else to examine before starting working on the fearful dog's triggers is the equipment used. Many people still walk their dogs with the lead attached to a flat collar. From a physiological standpoint, especially in a dog that might lunge towards a trigger, this can risk injury to the dog's neck and throat. There have been cases of the trachea (windpipe) being injured to the point of collapse. For this reason, the use of harnesses is recommended. Avoid the type with a strap that runs straight across the chest, instead using one that has an 'X' or 'Y' shaped section at the front. These allow full shoulder movement and do not hinder the dog's action in any way. When purchasing for a reactive dog a harness with front and rear rings is useful. Using a double-ended training lead to have two points of contact at the chest and on the back will mean confidence that you have a good, secure hold on your dog. The front ring means that turning the dog away from the trigger may be easier, leading to a better chance of being able to make a quick getaway. Ensure that the harness is not an 'anti-pull' harness as these are generally aversive by definition. Quality harnesses are not cheap but consider it as an investment in your dog's health and well-being.

Muzzles are often a divisive subject among dog guardians. The ability to wear a muzzle without problems is a valuable one, as it removes one element of stress from visits to the veterinary surgery. A muzzle can also give a dog guardian confidence to take their dog out in public as he cannot be accused of trying to bite, as some people may think when faced with a dog reacting to a trigger. Some guardians are concerned that other people will judge them due to the dog needing a muzzle, but the positives outweigh the negatives. Most dogs can happily adjust to wearing a muzzle with a little work and some tasty treats.

But how will my dog get exercise if he's not being walked?

Physical exercise is only part of the equation when it comes to any dog. Mental exercise can be very tiring, and taking advantage of this to give a break from going out for a walk means not having to worry about an under stimulated dog climbing the walls! Stretching your dog's brain can involve training sessions in the house or garden at home, or finding ways for him to work for his food. There are a wide range of toys that can be bought for dispensing food, such as Kongs® or forage mats amongst many others. This can become very expensive if you like to rotate your dog's toys to ensure they do not become boring. With a little imagination and a bit of effort, homemade versions of a number of these toys can be made, saving a lot of money. It is worth investing in a few good commercial enrichment toys, particularly those able be filled with a variety of different foods and then possibly frozen, as these give a multitude of options in terms of taste and texture. Around using these, there are countless options. An internet search for homemade enrichment for dogs will soon provide a list of ideas, ranging from the very simple such as a muffin tin and some tennis balls, to how to make your own fleece mats to hide food in and more. A perennial favourite in this house is kibble hidden inside an old cardboard box filled with toilet roll tubes. Once all the kibble is found, creating a snowfall of torn cardboard is loads of fun! There are so, so many ways of exercising dogs' brains, and problem solving is empowering for them just as it is for us.

Training at home can tire a dog mentally as well.

Sessions are best kept short, maybe ten minutes two or three times a day, to avoid the dog becoming bored and frustrated. This time can be used to work on behaviours that may help when in the outside world. Examples of these include reinforcing heelwork, teaching something like 'middle' where your dog will come and stand or sit between your legs on command (very useful for stopping people reaching to pet your dog when you do not wish them to) and working on impulse control. One tool that comes in very useful for impulse control is a flirt pole. This lure on the end of a stick and line can make for a great chase game, as you can drag it along the ground or throw the toy in the air for the dog to chase and catch, allowing them to display natural behaviours. It can equally be helpful for coaching your dog to wait on one spot despite the lure moving until released to chase it, so also potentially helping with prey drive and chasing behaviour.

With a bit of imagination and some DIY skills, you can make some agility equipment for the garden. A set of weave poles that go into the ground using spikes are not just useful for weaves. It is possible to buy some little pole holding cups and attached them to some of the poles to make jump stands, using a few of the remaining weave poles to make jumps. This exercise is great for practicing close control and directional commands, impulse control and patience with the initial wait. Be wary of overdoing jumping, whether in size, repetition or when the dog is very young as any of these could result in joint issues. A flat, stable surface such as a low table can also be very good for targeted waits and asking your dog to manoeuvre in different directions, which can be very useful when out walking. The table is ideal for directed placing of the paws, either front or back. An internet search for dog parkour gives some ideas for exercises which you and your dog can do together, which will help strengthen the bond between dog and guardian. The stronger the bond, the more your dog is likely to trust you when encountering the things that scare him.

One behaviour that can be vital when dealing with a reactive dog is asking them to focus on the handler. When focusing on the guardian, the dog simply cannot be fixated on the scary thing. Some people choose to ask their dogs to look at them, such as the 'Watch me' command, although that can be confrontational to a lot of dogs, particularly when considering using it in a situation that may already be somewhat stressful. For some dogs, another form of focusing can be preferable, such as having to touch their nose or a paw to something. In terms of my own reactive dog, he has been coached to 'mark' with his nose, touching it to my hand or alternatively some other target I point to while giving him the cue. When using a hand, it can be held in a variety of ways and positions so that the dog has to work out a way to touch the palm, using his ingenuity and environment to help him succeed.

Standard obedience cues have their place in coaching, and can be worked on during these home training sessions. Remember to vary the commands regularly, and mix them up to avoid boredom and staleness. Combining heelwork, sits and downs if they are important to you, and stays with other cues gives variety and interest to the session. Not every cue that you coach your dog in has to be 'useful' either. Coaching a spin, or roll over adds even more variety. Teach your dog to 'help' with the housework, to open cupboard doors or retrieve laundry from the washing machine.

There are so many things that you can do at home and coach your dog into success. All these fun, mentally and emotionally rewarding training sessions really strengthen the bond between handler and dog, which is at the core of helping the fearful dog be able to deal with life in the outside world. Make the sessions short and fun, and set your dog up to succeed. If any dog becomes frustrated during a training session, do not blame the dog. Examine what you are trying to do. Has the dog successfully completed this task before? Are you asking for too big a change in one go? If in doubt, ask your dog to complete a behaviour he knows well and can do easily, to ensure that the session ends happily all round.

Once the cortisol has had a chance to leave the dog's system, and he has returned to a baseline normal emotional state, then it is possible to begin working on the fear.

Desensitisation

This technique works well with dogs that are scared of noises, such as fireworks or thunderstorms. CDs or mp3s are available of the types of noise that dogs may typically find frightening. These can then be played at a very low volume in the dog's home. Start on an extremely low setting, and pair the time that the sound is playing with something the dog finds very rewarding, whether that is a high value food, a game with a favourite toy or fuss and attention from his guardian. If at any point the dog seems distracted by the noise and is unwilling to take the treats or engage with the game then the volume is too loud, and you need to go back a few steps to a quieter volume. Only when the dog seems entirely comfortable with the current volume should it increase. Any signs of hesitation or discomfort mean going back a couple of volume levels and allowing the comfort to return before again attempting to increase the volume.

It is important to note that although this technique can greatly help the dog in becoming accustomed to noises, there might be other factors surrounding the issue. Fireworks come with bright lights suddenly appearing in the sky. With thunderstorms, there may be pressure changes of which humans might only be dimly aware. It may not be possible to completely tackle the fear surrounding these, but by lessening the association between the noise and the frightening situation, we can hopefully give our dogs an easier time.

Another technique, which may help with these factors we cannot control, is the anxiety wrap. This applies gentle, consistent compression, which can aid many dogs in remaining calm in stressful situations. They are available to purchase commercially, and the website of the Thundershirt claims an eighty per cent success rate with a large number of positive reviews. A DIY version can be made at home using an elasticated compression bandage. Take a bandage suitable for your size of dog – narrow for a small dog, wide for a large one. Place the centre of the bandage across the dog's chest. Cross the sides of the bandage over the dog's shoulders, then again under his stomach and bring the ends up to his back again, tying them facing away from his spine. If you do not have a bandage but have a long scarf, you can also use this to create the makeshift anxiety wrap. One word of warning – never leave a dog unattended when wearing a wrap due to the danger of becoming entangled, although, hopefully a scared dog is not knowingly being left alone anyway. This technique is definitely worth trying as a drug free option. If it does not work for your dog, then it may be time to have a chat with your vet about medication to help keep your dog calm during the stressful occasions.

Counter conditioning

Conditioning is a process that dogs go through all of the time. Classical conditioning is learning by association, famously detailed in the story of Pavlov's dogs who began to salivate at the sound of a bell. We use operant conditioning in dog training all of the time, by applying consequences to behaviours that our dogs offer. In the case of positive, force free coaching, we use the positive reinforcement quadrant to encourage the behaviours that we want repeated.

Conditioning can happen without a conscious effort on our part. One simple to understand example is the dog attacked out on a walk by another, unknown dog. That one traumatic event can cause a long-standing issue, known as single event learning. One event of being attacked causes the poor victim to associate dogs he does not know with being attacked and so react to their approach with fear and overt defensive displays: reactivity.

The aim of counter conditioning is to change this negative association to a positive one. This is done with the aid of positive reinforcement, to change the dog's emotional response to the trigger. To do this, find the highest value treat to your dog. The dog decides what constitutes a high value treat, just as the dog decides what is aversive and that he does not like. To some, slivers of ham or cheese are something they will do anything to gain. For others it may be a particular toy. Whatever your dog finds the most rewarding thing ever must be reserved and only used for the counter conditioning exercise. For most dogs, this is usually food, and so food will be the reward in describing the technique.

As soon as the trigger comes into sight, but before the dog has a chance to react, start feeding the high value treats. If the dog fixates and stares at the trigger, or is not able to take the treats then the trigger is too close and you must increase the distance. Always start with as much distance as you can manage and gradually work closer. Keeping feeding constantly for the entire time the trigger is in sight. To make this easier, some people choose to use 'squeezy cheese' that comes in a tube. There are a variety of flavours to pick which one your dog likes best (ham is a favourite with my reactive dog) and it is easy to dispense with one hand while the other is holding the lead. This form of cheese also has the advantage that a small squeeze will have them licking the nozzle for a long time, so the calorie content is not too high. As soon as the trigger goes out of sight, the high value treat immediately goes away. It is only available when the scary thing is near. Over time, the fearful dog will start to look for the goodies when the trigger comes into view rather than reacting. As this happens, the distance can decrease bringing the trigger slowly closer. If at any time the fearful dog reacts, increase the distance and slow down the progress.

This is not a quick process but, done correctly, it can be very effective. You can perform the technique whenever you encounter a trigger out on a walk; provided you can get enough distance for your dog to comfortably take treats. A useful cue to coach during those at home training sessions is a bright, breezy 'This way!' with lots of enthusiasm and reward, so that if you suddenly come across a trigger, you can ask your dog to turn and head the other way rapidly, and hopefully avoiding too much stress.

BAT

BAT stands for Behaviour Adjustment Training, and is the creation of Grisha Stewart. A wonderfully empowering technique, BAT teaches and allows the dog to make choices about their environment. A BAT trained dog has the ability to be proactive, to choose calm behaviours. It relies heavily on communication between dog and handler, and so builds a great amount of trust and confidence between the two. It does require an amount of reading and study before the novice handler can start using BAT techniques with their dog, but much advice is available on Grisha Stewart's website found at grishastewart.com/why-try-bat/ or in her book Behaviour Adjustment Training 2.0, also available on the website or in a wide range of book selling locations. If not confident to try using this technique alone, the website holds a directory of certified BAT instructors, searchable by location.

If in any doubt whether you can comfortably use any of these techniques yourself, find a good positive force free trainer to help you and your fearful dog.

9 PREVENTION OVER CURE

It is easy to think that the way to avoid reactivity is to get a puppy. All reactive dogs must have come from bad homes, or been mistreated in some way for them to be fearful, after all.

Sadly, it is not that simple.

My own reactive dog has been with me since the age of eight weeks old. He has never experienced mistreatment in that time and yet, around the age of sixteen weeks, he started showing signs of developing reactivity. At that time, I knew nothing about the subject and so missed the early signs, and had no idea how to help his issues as time progressed, or even to what extent I could help them at all. Some factors contributing to reactivity and fearfulness we can affect, but others we cannot. In order to work out which are open to improvement, we must look at the contributors to reactivity in dogs.

As in all things when it comes to living organisms, genetics dictate the basic structure of the dog from the moment of conception. Due to the way in which reproductive cells come into being and the genetic material of the parent animals split between them, every single puppy is a unique individual, even those born in the same litter. Reproductive cells multiply in a two-stage process called meiosis, and this double division of the genetic input is what creates such a wide variety of possible combinations from the parent DNA. In the first stage, the DNA is copied and then splits to each side of the cell at random before it divides, ensuring that every mixture (with the exception of identical twins) is unique. This results in two cells, which then split again to result in four 'daughter cells', each containing half of the genetic code required for life. These daughter cells are the gametes, better known as the sperm and egg cells of the reproductive system. When an egg is fertilised by a sperm cell, the amount of genetic material is full again. In the case of dogs, this means thirty-nine pairs of chromosomes are fused and set at conception and cannot change.

Studies have shown that fearful parent animals can tend towards producing fearful offspring, showing that a genetic component to fear exists. This is not something that we as guardians can affect, as the genes are set once conception has occurred, but it is a factor to keep in mind when assessing a potential puppy along with their parents.

That is an important note: when searching for a puppy to join your family, careful breeder selection is vital. For a puppy to have the best chance of a happy family life with minimal stress, the conditions in which the mother carries the puppies, they are whelped and raised all have huge connotations for their future health and happiness.

When looking to buy a puppy, it is so important to make sure that there is no chance you are buying the product of a puppy farm setup. These 'conveyor belt' production mills treat the parent dogs as commodities, keeping them in cramped, stressful surroundings. Health testing is likely to be minimal if it exists at all, and the mothers and puppies spend their days in small pens, with little in the way of comfort or any kind of enrichment. Puppy farmers are extremely unlikely to take proper care of the mother or puppies' health, with worming or flea treatments probably skimped on. Socialisation may well be non-existent. As discussed in previous chapters, constant stress like that suffered by the mother is going to have a detrimental effect on her physical, psychological and mental health. Also, remember that the puppies' bloodstream links to the mother's via the umbilical cord and placenta, and so the stress hormones in the mother's bloodstream can pass through to the puppies. This means that, while still in the uterus, the puppies are developing prepared to enter a stressful world. This means that they are much more likely to be fearful and show fearful and reactive behaviours.

Aside from the very valid ethical concerns that surround puppy farming, add also the lack of health care, socialisation and strong chance that the puppy could be ill when sold. Puppies tend to look healthy even when they are not, and the puppy farm method means a high risk that the pup will be carrying some form of illness. The reasons for not spending your money perpetuating these places are easy to see. A puppy from a reputable, ethical breeder will have a higher purchase price, but is less likely to incur high vet bills early in life. There are no guarantees when it comes to young animals, but a much better start in life will help to minimise the risks of illness, and the feeling of losing a beloved family member young when they should have had a long and happy life in front of them is indescribable.

A good, ethical breeder that is breeding because they love the breed and want to produce good healthy examples will raise the puppies in a home environment, exposing them to all the sights, sounds and smells of normal life in a human household. They will accustom the puppies to gentle, respectful handling while making sure neither puppy nor mother find the experience stressful. Good breeders will welcome questions to ensure that they find their puppies appropriate homes. They will allow you to visit mum and pups in the whelping environment so that you can see they are well raised. They will be happy for you to visit more than once. A large number of these great, ethical breeders will offer support and advice while the puppy is growing into a young dog, and many will take the pup back if something happens that means keeping the puppy is not a possibility. For instance, if a family member around dogs for the first time discovers they are severely allergic, or there is some kind of incompatibility between the puppy and a dog already in the household. A good potential dog guardian will have made sure as far as possible that a new puppy will fit into the home and that they can provide for his requirements outside of extreme unexpected circumstances.

Finding the right breeder is a big task and should not be hurried. Adding a canine family member is a commitment that lasts for upwards of ten years, hopefully several longer than that. Talk to your vet and friends that have dogs. If you favour a particular breed, contact the breed society, or have a look on the Kennel Club website to start to find possible breeders to contact. Once you have found a shortlist, start asking questions. A good breeder will be happy to answer, and may well have questions to ask you to ensure a harmonious match. Think very carefully before buying a puppy from the classifieds. If you do decide to source a puppy this way, make sure to ask many questions. If you are not able to visit and see the puppies with their mother, walk away. Never have a puppy delivered or agree to meet somewhere neutral for a handover. Both of these situations could easily be hiding the fact that you are purchasing a puppy from a puppy farm setup.

Once you have got your puppy and brought him safely home, now the hard work begins!

It is a misconception that puppies are easy. Puppies are cute, mischievous and one of the most adorably glorious time wasters on the planet (not that any dog is ever a waste of time, but most people cannot pass a puppy without wanting to spend a serious amount of time with them) but the one thing they are not is easy. There is a saying that the first twelve months of a dog's life are an investment in their future health and happiness, and this is quite accurate. The rate at which a puppy grows physically is easy to see, as they seem to change every day. Mental growth is also rapid, but the period of time in which we can affect and have a permanent positive effect on the dog's outlook on life, and his attitude towards meeting new things, is very short.

This period in which the dog's mental perspective develops to create a happy, well-balanced adult individual is the critical socialisation period. It is an early part of the dog's lifespan, running from approximately three and a half weeks to at most fourteen weeks. The exact time at which the socialisation period ends varies between breeds and individuals. As always, individuality is a huge factor. Because the end does not occur on an easily recognisable fixed point, many people recommend ensuring that your puppy is widely socialised by the age of twelve weeks. However, a number of issues can interfere with the socialisation process.

The subject of vaccinations can be very divisive among dog guardians and professionals. The dangers of over vaccination have come much to the fore in recent years, and vaccination protocols are frequently a matter of much debate. What is not under debate is the necessity of the full course of puppy vaccinations. Puppies have initial protection due to the antibodies they receive from their mother via the placenta and colostrum in their first feeds at under eighteen hours old. These maternal antibodies will be in the bloodstream at a high level to begin with, and would stop any vaccinations from working by destroying the foreign invaders. The level of maternal antibodies drops as the puppies grow older, but the point at which the level drops low enough for a vaccination to work is impossible to ascertain. This is why the puppy protocol involves multiple vaccinations a short period apart. There is a time in which protection from the maternal antibodies drops and before the vaccinations received at the veterinary surgery have prompted the puppy's immune system to develop fully. This is the window of susceptibility, the period in which a puppy is at elevated risk of contracting disease. This is the reason that vets tell guardians to keep their dogs at home until the last vaccination in the puppy course will have had a chance to work.

The problem with this advice is that the time puppies receive their vaccinations is right at the time when guardians need to be working on socialising their young charge. Many follow the advice of their vet in good faith, without realising there is a way around the problem. Puppies can get out and see a lot of the world without encountering disease risk. Carry them so that they can experience sights, sounds and smells. Alternatively, some people use buggies to wheel their puppies around on longer walks, and one of these may prove useful if they get tired adventuring. If you are in an area not frequented by a large number of dogs, let him have a run around and explore his new world. Arrange meetups with friends or family that have fully vaccinated dogs of a suitable temperament so that your pup can learn appropriate social skills and body language from other dogs while minimising risk. Let him meet as wide a variety of people as possible, of all ages and appearances. Introduce him to children in buggies, people walking with sticks, or in wheelchairs, people wearing hats, men with beards.

Expose your puppy to as many different situations as possible also, so that he sees different vehicles on the road and livestock in the fields. Take him for rides in the car, and not just ones that end at the veterinary surgery! Take him to visit new places or just out for a ride around. Familiarity is the best way to battle the carsickness that young pups often experience at first. Work on giving him the best experiences possible so that he comes to view getting in the car as a great, positive experience.

Once the vaccinations are completed and the puppy's immune system fully developed, he can start introductions to more dogs. Be sure to check that these dogs are temperamentally suited to meeting young puppies, as a bite or frightening experience at a young age can lead to later dog reactivity. For safety, never leave your puppy unsupervised with any other dog, particularly one bigger than him. That runs the risk of predatory drift, when the larger dog could lose the inhibition that they have learned over generations to stop ritualised play turning into the instinctive compulsion to follow through on the predatory behaviour. Even without the risk of predatory drift, a larger dog could potentially injure a puppy in the course of normal play. Even if the injury is not serious or long lasting, it could lead to the puppy starting to be wary of other dogs.

The mistake a lot of people make with socialisation is forcing their puppies into situations without ensuring that they are happy or, even worse, laugh at the puppy's fearful behaviour because they don't know any better. If a puppy shows any kind of fear, such as distance creating behaviours like hiding behind their guardian, height seeking by trying to climb or get themselves picked up, or fear aggressive behaviours like growling or displaying teeth, or urinating in extreme cases, then the attempt at socialisation must be abandoned immediately. Forcing the issue will only backfire and create a fear association that was not already in place, potentially leading to reactivity. Learning as much as possible about canine body language will help greatly in knowing whether the situation is being pressed too far, and the dog would benefit from backing off at that moment.

A well-socialised puppy will grow into a happy and confident adult dog. As many dog guardians know, it is impossible to guarantee that nothing will ever happen to cause a dog to become reactive, but by taking the time and effort to socialise him well, his guardian can know that they have done the best job they possibly can by him.

Experiences play a large part in determining reactivity, and can happen at any point in the dog's life to cause difficulty. This is where the dog guardian has to accept that they cannot control everything that happens to their dogs. We share our world and our environment with a huge number of other people, their lifestyles, vehicles and pets. It is possible that a dog guardian can do an amazing job of raising and socialising their puppy but all of that work is potentially ruined by an out of control, off-lead dog that crowds them and doesn't read their signals requesting space, or a car drives past very close and fast, spooking them. All we can do is our best, to give them the very best start in life that we can to instil resilience, so that they can encounter these difficulties with the minimum of psychological trauma possible.

ABOUT THE AUTHOR

Jay has been working with and training dogs with more enthusiasm than skill for more years than she cares to remember, largely working Border Collies (or in the case of one very determined dog, NOT working). Although no longer living on the farm or farming sheep, the Border Collie has wormed its way into her heart enough to still be the dog of choice. It was the younger of her current dogs that caused her having to research reactivity and, in the process, discover a new love of learning about dog training and behaviour. A lifelong love affair with the written word has combined with the new interest to inspire her attempt to ensure that no reactive dog owner needs to feel that they are alone.

Printed in Great Britain
by Amazon